IMPACT!

Adult
Literacy
and
Language
Skills

Book 1

Janice C. Motta
Reading Specialist
Dean of Continuing Education
Bristol Community College

Kathryn L. Riley
ESL Specialist
Coordinator of ESL Program
Roxbury Community College

▲ **ADDISON-WESLEY PUBLISHING COMPANY**
Reading, Massachusetts • Menlo Park, California • Don Mills, Ontario
Amsterdam • London • Manila • Singapore • Sydney • Tokyo

for Joseph F. Motta
Hazel P. Riley

ABCDEFGHIJ-AL-8987654321
ISBN: 0-201-05310-1

TO THE TEACHER

Impact! is a three-level ESL reading skills development program designed to be used in conjunction with any ESL series. *Impact!* is also a powerful teaching tool to use with native speakers who need to master reading skills. The program uses a sight word approach tested and proven most effective with adult beginning readers. *Impact!* is unique in that it guarantees success to students by controlling grade level, grammatical structures, and required reading skills, while presenting adult topics and survival vocabulary to ensure motivation. Numerous illustrations provide helpful context clues for understanding vocabulary. Writing, speaking, and listening skills are integrated into the program as well.

Book 1 of *Impact!* is intended for students who already possess prereading skills. These students should also understand the concept of print as a written representation of speech, be capable of discriminating between like and unlike words, and have practiced the left-to-right, top-to-bottom eye movement necessary for reading in English.

It is crucial to the successful use of *Impact!* that the vocabulary and grammar be taught orally and in meaningful context before students begin each lesson. As an aid to teaching vocabulary, use the detailed illustration at the beginning of each lesson in Book 1 of *Impact!* In most cases, the grammar structures will be reinforcing grammar work learned through the ESL series being used in the class. Spend time working orally with students to be sure that they feel comfortable using the vocabulary and grammar in each lesson. Do not begin the reading lesson until the vocabulary and grammar have been mastered orally. (How to accomplish these goals is fully explained in the Teacher's Guide.)

Use of the Teacher's Guide for Book 1 of *Impact!* is recommended. It provides step-by-step directions, as well as follow-up and enrichment activities, for effective use of the student text. In addition, the Teacher's Guide features answer keys, lesson-by-lesson charts of ESL and reading structures, and discussion ideas.

CONTENTS

Lessons

Lesson One

OUR STREET

a	birth	house	man	street
address	date	husband	my	telephone
age	from	I	name	this
am	he	I'm	number	we
an	her	in	our	wife
are	his	is	she	woman
		living		

Write:

a _____

address _____

age _____

am _____

an _____

are _____

birth _____

date _____

from _____

he _____

her _____

his _____

house _____

husband _____

I _____

I'm _____

in _____

is _____

living _____

man _____

my _____

name _____

number _____

our _____

she _____

street _____

telephone _____

this _____

we _____

wife _____

woman _____

Phrases

an address

my birth date

in a house

our street

this man

her husband

his wife

a telephone number

my age

a woman

her name

Write:

an address _____

my birth date _____

in a house _____

our street _____

this man _____

her husband _____

his wife _____

a telephone number _____

my age _____

a woman _____

her name _____

Sentences

1. I am a woman.
2. My age is 30.
3. My name is Anna.

4. I'm a man.
5. I'm his wife.
6. We are living in a house.

7. He is from America.
8. She is from Mexico.
9. He is her husband.

Write:

2. _____

6. _____

7. _____

OUR STREET

My name is Joe. I am a man. This is my wife. Her name is Rose. She is a woman. We are living in a house. Our address is 521 Main Street. Our telephone number is 231-8145.

I am from Cuba. I'm a Cuban. My age is 50. My birth date is May 5, 1932. My wife is from America. She is an American. Her birth date is June 8, 1934. Her age is 48.

My name is Anna. I am a woman. This is my husband. His name is Jim. He is a man. We are living in a house. Our address is 523 Main Street. Our telephone number is 231-7602.

I am from Mexico. I am a Mexican. My age is 30. My birth date is May 21, 1952. My husband is from America. He is an American. His birth date is June 21, 1950. His age is 32.

Exercise 1: Match and Check — Phrases

Directions: Check (√) the right answer. Write the right answer.

1.
   - ( ) a street
   - ( ) my wife
   - ( ) a man

   Write: _____ *a man* _____

2. Anna
   - ( ) his age
   - ( ) a name
   - ( ) a telephone

   Write: _____

3.
   - ( ) a house
   - ( ) a woman
   - ( ) a husband

   Write: _____

4. 231 - 7602
   - ( ) a telephone number
   - ( ) an address
   - ( ) a name

   Write: _____

5. 521 Main Street
   - ( ) an address
   - ( ) a birth date
   - ( ) his wife

   Write: _____

Exercise 2: Match and Check — Sentences

Directions: Check (√) the right answer. Write the right answer.

1.

( ) His age is 2.

( ) My age is 50.

( ) He is a man.

Write: _____

2.

( ) She is living in a house.

( ) Her telephone number is 520-1253.

( ) He is living in a house.

Write: _____

3.

( ) My name is Joe.

( ) My age is 16.

( ) This is a street.

Write: _____

4.

MAY 5, 1947

( ) This is her age.

( ) This is her birth date.

( ) I am American.

Write: _____

Exercise 3: Letter Words

Directions: Write the words with the same first letter.

he
I
a
her
address
age
telephone
I'm
am
this
in
an
his
are
house
is
husband

a

_a_

_____

_____

_____

_____

_____

_____

t

telephone

h

_he_

_____

_____

_____

_____

_____

i

_I_

_____

_____

_____

Exercise 4: THINK

Directions: This exercise is about you. Fill in the blanks.

1. My name is _____ .

2. My address is _____ .

3. My telephone number is _____ .

4. My birth date is _____ .

5. My age is _____ .

Lesson Two

2

THE FAMILY

and	mother	son-in-law
brother	mother-in-law	their
brother-in-law	no	they
daughter	parents	they're
family	she's	to
father	single	with
father-in-law	sister	yes
married	son	

Write:

and _____   she's _____

brother _____   single _____

brother-in-law _____   sister _____

daughter _____   son _____

family _____   son-in-law _____

father _____   their _____

father-in-law _____   they _____

married _____   they're _____

mother _____   to _____

mother-in-law _____   with _____

no _____   yes _____

parents _____

Phrases

my son-in-law   a single sister   his daughter
yes and no   their family   with my mother-in-law
their parents   to her brother   to her father-in-law

Write:

my son-in-law _____

yes and no _____

their parents _____

a single sister _____

their family _____

to her brother _____

his daughter _____

with my mother-in-law _____

to her father-in-law _____

Sentences

1. They are married.

2. They're parents.

3. They are a mother and a father.

4. He's a brother.

5. He's a brother-in-law.

6. He's a son.

7. Her age is 21.

8. She's single.

9. She's a daughter.

Write:

1. _____

5. _____

9. _____

THE FAMILY

Pat Bates is married. She's with her husband. His name is Dave. They're living with her family. Her parents are Mary and Dan Woods. Her brother is Jack Woods.

Mary and Dan Woods are married. Jack Woods is their son. Pat Bates is their daughter. Dave Bates is their son-in-law.

Jack is single. He's 19. Dan is his father. Mary is his mother. Pat Bates is his sister. Dave Bates is his brother-in-law.

Dave is married to Pat. Mary Woods is his mother-in-law. Dan is his father-in-law. Jack is his brother-in-law.

They are living in a house. Their address is 352 Elm Street. Their telephone number is 251-8970.

Exercise 1: Match and Check — Phrases

Directions: Check (√) the right answer. Write the right answer.

1.

( ) my parents

( ) with my father

( ) with my wife

Write: _____

2.

( ) a single man

( ) our address

( ) a married woman

Write: _____

3.

( ) a family

( ) in a house

( ) my telephone

Write: _____

4.

( ) their brother-in-law

( ) their daughter

( ) his mother

Write: _____

5.

( ) with my mother-in-law

( ) his street

( ) with my daughter-in-law

Write: _____

Exercise 2: Match and Check — Sentences

Directions: Check (√) the right answer. Write the right answer.

1.
( ) He is single.

( ) This is my mother-in-law.

( ) Jane is a Cuban.

Write: _____

2.
( ) His birth date is July 13, 1980.

( ) My father is with my mother.

( ) He is with my father-in-law.

Write: _____

3.
( ) They are 16.

( ) They are with their daughter.

( ) They're my parents.

Write: _____

4.
( ) He's living with his brother.

( ) She's living with her brother.

( ) His parents are in a house.

Write: _____

Exercise 3: Letter Words

Directions: Write the words with the same first letter.

family
brother
married
she's
mother
father
mother-in-law
brother-in-law
single
father-in-law
sister
son
son-in-law

m

married

f

family

s

she's

b

brother

✳Exercise 4: THINK

Directions: This exercise is about you. Circle the right answer.

1.	I am married.	yes	no
2.	I am a mother.	yes	no
3.	I am single.	yes	no
4.	I am a father.	yes	no
5.	I am living with my parents.	yes	no
6.	I am a woman.	yes	no
7.	I am a parent.	yes	no
8.	I am a daughter-in-law.	yes	no
9.	I am a man.	yes	no
10.	I am 21.	yes	no
11.	I am from Mexico.	yes	no

Lesson Three

3

THE APARTMENT BUILDING

above	cooking	it's	student
apartment	divorced	landlord	studying
bedroom	four	now	the
below	grandmother	old	there
big	here	one	three
building	he's	playing	two
cat	it	renting	young
cleaning			

Write:

above _____ it's _____

apartment _____ landlord _____

bedroom _____ now _____

below _____ old _____

big _____ one _____

building _____ playing _____

cat _____ renting _____

cleaning _____ student _____

cooking _____ studying _____

divorced _____ the _____

four _____ there _____

grandmother _____ three _____

here _____ two _____

he's _____ young _____

it _____

21

Phrases

four students
here and there
above the big building
below the apartment

my landlord
a divorced woman
one cat

two bedrooms
my old address
three daughters

Write:

four students _____

here and there _____

above the big building _____

below the apartment _____

my landlord _____

a divorced woman _____

one cat _____

two bedrooms _____

my old address _____

three daughters _____

Sentences

1. She's cooking now.

2. He's cleaning.

3. She's a grandmother.

4. He's renting an apartment.

5. He's studying.

6. He's a student.

7. It is a cat.

8. It's a young cat.

9. It's playing.

Write:

3. _____

4. _____

7. _____

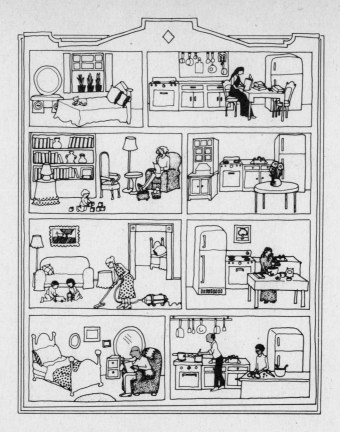

THE APARTMENT BUILDING

This is my building. It is in New York. I am the landlord. There are four apartments in my building.

Mr. and Mrs. Roma are renting Apartment 2. It is a three-bedroom apartment. It's a big family. They are from Italy. They're Italian. Mrs. Roma is cooking now. Her sons are playing. Their grandmother is cleaning. She is old. She is 78.

Mrs. Geer is renting Apartment 3. It is above Apartment 2. It's a two-bedroom apartment. She is living with her son. His name is Ned. He is young. He is four. His father is living in California. Mrs. Geer is divorced. She is single now.

Mona is renting Apartment 4. It is above Apartment 3. It's a one-bedroom apartment. She is from India. She's Indian. Mona is a student. She's studying now. She's single. She is living with her cat.

I am living in Apartment 1. It's below Apartment 2. It's a two-bedroom apartment. I'm married. I'm living with my wife. My father is living here. He's old. He's 79.

Exercise 1: Match and Check — Phrases

Directions: Check (√) the right answer. Write the right answer.

1.

    ( )   three cats

    ( )   above an apartment

    ( )   two young sons

    Write: _____

2.

    ( )   in a bedroom

    ( )   my landlord

    ( )   a telephone

    Write: _____

3.

    ( )   two apartments

    ( )   four students

    ( )   a house

    Write: _____

4.

    ( )   one grandmother

    ( )   her telephone

    ( )   two students

    Write: _____

5.

    ( )   three sisters

    ( )   a big building

    ( )   cleaning my apartment

    Write: _____

Exercise 2: Match and Check — Sentences

Directions: Check (√) the right answer. Write the right answer.

1.

    ( ) Her husband is old.

    ( ) My father is cleaning the apartment.

    ( ) She's renting the apartment.

    Write: _____

2.

    ( ) They're playing in the street.

    ( ) It's an old building.

    ( ) He's married.

    Write: _____

3.

    ( ) His grandmother is cooking.

    ( ) The cats are playing.

    ( ) She's young.

    Write: _____

4.

    ( ) The young girls are playing.

    ( ) My brother is divorced.

    ( ) The young girls are studying.

    Write: _____

Exercise 3: Letter Words

Directions: Write the words with the same first letter.

bedroom
cat
below
one
cleaning
the
big
old
there
cooking
our
building
three
two

c	o
cat	*one*

t	b
the	*bedroom*

☀ Exercise 4: THINK

Directions: This exercise is about you. Circle the right answer.

1. I am studying now.	yes	no
2. I am a landlord.	yes	no
3. I am divorced.	yes	no
4. I am living in a two-bedroom apartment.	yes	no
5. I am a student.	yes	no
6. I am cooking now.	yes	no
7. I am living with my grandmother.	yes	no
8. I am young.	yes	no
9. I am old.	yes	no
10. I am living in New York.	yes	no

Lesson Four

28

THE OFFICE BUILDING

at	fourth	on	third
basement	girls	restaurant	today
boss	giving	second	typing
clerks	janitor	secretary	waiter
desk	medicine	sitting	waitress
doctor	nurse	tables	working
first	office	talking	writing
floor			

Write:

at _____

basement _____

boss_____

clerks_____

desk _____

doctor _____

first_____

floor _____

fourth _____

girls_____

giving _____

janitor _____

medicine_____

nurse _____

office _____

on _____

restaurant _____

second_____

secretary _____

sitting _____

tables _____

talking _____

third _____

today _____

typing _____

waiter _____

waitress_____

working_____

writing _____

Phrases

a doctor and a nurse   fourth floor
second floor   my boss
at the table   the basement
one janitor   three girls
in the restaurant   a waiter and a waitress

Write:

a doctor and a nurse _____

second floor_____

at the table _____

one janitor _____

in the restaurant _____

fourth floor _____

my boss _____

the basement_____

three girls_____

a waiter and a waitress _____

Sentences

1. The secretary is typing.

2. The clerk is writing.

3. The boss is sitting at his desk.

4. The waiter and waitress are working in the restaurant today.

5. The restaurant is on the first floor.

6. The girls are talking.

7. The nurse is writing.

8. The doctor is giving medicine to a man.

9. Their office is on the third floor.

Write:

3. _____

5. _____

8. _____

THE OFFICE BUILDING

I am a janitor. My office is in the basement. Today I am cleaning the building. My name is Steve.

Ann Black is a waitress. Fred Adams is a waiter. They are working in Bill's Restaurant. It is on the first floor. They are cleaning tables.

Dan Potter is a doctor. His office is on the second floor. He is giving medicine to a girl. Pam Reed is his nurse. She is talking to two girls.

Liz Kane is a secretary. Her office is on the third floor. She is typing. Her boss is Bob Jones. He is sitting at his desk. He is writing.

Tom and Dick are clerks. Their office is on the fourth floor. Tom is typing. Dick is talking on the telephone.

There are four floors in the building.

Exercise 1: Match and Check — Phrases

Directions: Check (✓) the right answer. Write the right answer.

1.
( ) writing at a desk

( ) typing in an office

( ) one waiter

Write:_____

2.
( ) talking on the telephone

( ) cleaning the tables

( ) talking to the nurse

Write: _____

3.
( ) the janitor and the waitress

( ) sitting in an office

( ) the doctor and the nurse

Write: _____

4.
( ) studying in her apartment

( ) giving the medicine

( ) talking to the girls

Write: _____

5.
( ) an old doctor

( ) two clerks

( ) a young doctor

Write: _____

Exercise 2: Match and Check — Sentences

Directions: Check (√) the right answer. Write the right answer.

1. ( ) The secretary is talking on the telephone.

    ( ) The boss is talking to two girls.

    ( ) The janitors are working.

    Write: _____

2. ( ) The waiters are working.

    ( ) The girls are sitting.

    ( ) The clerks are typing.

    Write: _____

3. ( ) The janitor is working in the basement.

    ( ) The waitress is cleaning a table.

    ( ) Her boss is working at his desk.

    Write: _____

4. ( ) There are three floors in this building.

    ( ) Jim and Sue are clerks.

    ( ) This is our house.

    Write: _____

34

Exercise 3: Letter Words

Directions: Write the words with the same first letter.

tables
girls
waiter
desk
talking
waitress
third
giving
doctor
working
today
writing
typing

t
tables

d
desk

w
waiter

g
girls

Exercise 4: THINK

Directions: Find the right word. Fill in the blanks.

doctor	secretary	third	janitor
nurse	first	fourth	second

The _____ is first.

The _____ is second.

The _____ is third.

The _____ is fourth.

The doctor is _____ .

The nurse is _____ .

The janitor is _____ .

The secretary is _____ .

Check-Up Lessons 1–4

Exercise 1: Match and Check

Directions: Check (√) the right answer. Write the right answer.

1. ( ) a woman

   ( ) a man

   ( ) my son

   Write: _____

2. ( ) two students

   ( ) one grandmother

   ( ) three sisters

   Write: _____

3. ( ) talking on the telephone

   ( ) studying in her bedroom

   ( ) cleaning her apartment

   Write: _____

4. ( ) The waiter is cleaning the table.

   ( ) The janitor is working in the basement.

   ( ) The waitress is working.

   Write: _____

5.

( ) This is Jane.

( ) He is single.

( ) Her age is 12.

Write: _____

Exercise 2: Letter Words

Directions: Write the words with the same first letter.

	h	b
girls	_____	_____
cat	_____	_____
cleaning	_____	
brother-in-law		
house	_____	
giving	c	g
cooking	_____	_____
brother	_____	_____
he		
husband	_____	

Exercise 3: THINK

Directions: These sentences are about you. Circle the right answer.

1. I am studying now.   yes   no

2. I am a student.   yes   no

3. I am married.   yes   no

4. I am a father.   yes   no

5. I am living with my parents.   yes   no

Lesson Five

ELM STREET

across	firemen	next	sign
aren't	front	of	station
busy	going	parking	stop
car	isn't	police	store
clothing	liquor	police officer	supermarket
corner	men	post office	that's
fire	neighbor		

Write:

across _____

aren't_____

busy _____

car _____

clothing _____

corner _____

fire _____

firemen _____

front _____

going_____

isn't_____

liquor_____

men_____

neighbor _____

next _____

of_____

parking _____

police _____

police officer_____

post office _____

sign _____

station_____

stop _____

store _____

supermarket _____

that's _____

Phrases

a busy corner   across from the sign
a stop sign   my neighbor's car
the busy firemen   no parking
our police station   in front of the men
the clothing store   our supermarket
next to the post office

Write:

a busy corner _____

a stop sign _____

the busy firemen _____

our police station _____

the clothing store _____

next to the post office _____

across from the sign _____

my neighbor's car _____

no parking _____

in front of the men _____

our supermarket _____

Sentences

1. A police officer is talking to a girl in front of the police station.

2. That's our police station.

3. My neighbor is a police officer.

4. The fire station isn't big.

5. It's at the corner.

6. The firemen aren't sitting in front of it.

7. Two men are going in the liquor store.

8. The store isn't busy.

9. There's a NO PARKING sign in front of the store.

Write:

2. _____

4. _____

7. _____

ELM STREET

This is Elm Street. I am renting an apartment on this street. It is in the building next to the liquor store.

That's my neighbor Joe. He is parking his car. He isn't living in my building. He is renting the house next to the post office. Joe's son is a police officer. He is going in the police station. There is a NO PARKING sign in front of the police station. A police car is parking there now.

The fire station is at the corner of the street. There is a STOP sign at the corner. Two firemen are cleaning the building. They aren't at a fire now.

Brook's Restaurant is next to the fire station. It is a big restaurant. It's across the street from Sam's. Sam's is a clothing store. Two men are in the store. It isn't busy today.

There is a supermarket next to Sam's. It's busy. It is on the corner across from the fire station.

Exercise 1: Match and Check — Phrases

Directions: Check (√) the right answer. Write the right answer.

1.

( ) a busy store

( ) a police station

( ) a post office

Write: _____

2.

( ) on the corner of the street

( ) across the street

( ) playing in the street

Write: _____

3.

( ) next to the clothing store

( ) parking the car

( ) behind the STOP sign

Write: _____

4.

( ) a husband and wife

( ) talking to the men

( ) in the basement

Write: _____

5.

( ) a big building

( ) a telephone number

( ) at the restaurant

Write: _____

Exercise 2: Match and Check — Sentences

Directions: Check (√) the right answer. Write the right answer.

1. ( ) The police officer is parking his car.

   ( ) These men are my neighbors.

   ( ) My friend Anna is working.

   Write: _____

2. ( ) The fire station is on the corner.

   ( ) The firemen are going into the fire station.

   ( ) The children are playing in the street.

   Write: _____

3. ( ) The STOP sign is in front of the supermarket.

   ( ) The girls are sitting next to the building.

   ( ) The clerk is in the clothing store.

   Write: _____

4. ( ) That's a liquor store.

   ( ) These men are my neighbors.

   ( ) It's a supermarket.

   Write: _____

44

Exercise 3: Letter Words

Directions: Write the words with the same first letter.

fire
sign
parking
station
firemen
police
across
stop
store
police officer
aren't
supermarket
front
post office

p
parking
_____
_____
_____

f
fire
_____
_____

s
sign
_____
_____
_____

a
across
_____

Exercise 4: THINK

Directions: Where do they work? Write the answers.

clerk   nurse   waitress
doctor   secretary   firemen
janitor   waiter   police officer

fire station   *office building*
_____   _____

police station
_____   _____

restaurant
_____   _____

45

Lesson Six

IN A SUPERMARKET

apples	checkout	him	out
behind	chicken	inside	people
bread	coming	many	pound
buying	corn	meat	rice
cart	counter	milk	shopping
cash	eggs	not	soup
cashier	expensive	on	them
cheap	food		

Write:

apples _____

behind _____

bread _____

buying _____

cart _____

cash _____

cashier _____

cheap _____

checkout _____

chicken _____

coming _____

corn _____

counter _____

eggs _____

expensive _____

food _____

him _____

inside _____

many _____

meat _____

milk _____

not _____

on _____

out _____

people _____

pound _____

rice _____

shopping _____

soup _____

them _____

Phrases

behind a cart
the checkout counter
bread and eggs
expensive meat
a pound of apples

many people
cheap food
inside the supermarket
milk and soup
on the counter

Write:

behind a cart _____

the checkout counter _____

bread and eggs _____

expensive meat _____

a pound of apples _____

many people _____

cheap food _____

inside the supermarket _____

milk and soup _____

on the counter _____

Sentences

1. The cashier is behind the counter.

2. A man is buying a chicken and rice.

3. He is buying them with cash.

4. A man is shopping.

5. His son is with him.

6. They aren't going out.

7. Many people are shopping.

8. Their food is in their carts.

9. The food is expensive.

Write:

3. _____

5. _____

6. _____

IN A SUPERMARKET

This is a supermarket. It is busy today. There are many people inside. They are shopping. A woman is coming in. Two men are going out.

Ed is at the checkout counter. He is buying food. Jan is behind him. Her food is in her cart.

Ed's food is on the counter. The meat is first. It is $4.99 a pound. It's expensive. The apples are second. They are 29¢ a pound. They're not expensive. They're cheap.

The soup is next to the bread. The corn is behind the chicken. The rice is next to the chicken. The milk is in front of the eggs.

Ed is buying his food with cash. He is giving it to the cashier. She is working behind the counter. She is busy today.

Exercise 1: Match and Check — Phrases

Directions: Check (√) the right answer. Write the right answer.

1.
( ) a pound of rice

( ) many apples

( ) chicken and meat

Write: _____

2.
( ) in the shopping cart

( ) on the counter

( ) behind the cashier

Write: _____

3.
( ) in the liquor store

( ) next to the supermarket

( ) in front of the restaurant

Write: _____

4.
( ) coming out

( ) going in

( ) inside the clothing store

Write: _____

5.
( ) buying food

( ) expensive meat

( ) in the shopping cart

Write: _____

Exercise 2: Match and Check — Sentences

Directions: Check (√) the right answer. Write the right answer.

1. ( ) He is going to the supermarket.

   ( ) The men aren't in front of the super-market.

   ( ) He is coming out of the supermarket.

   Write: _____

2. ( ) The woman is buying the bread with cash.

   ( ) He isn't buying them for his parents.

   ( ) She is buying chicken.

   Write: _____

3. ( ) The cashier is behind the checkout counter.

   ( ) She is giving him the cash.

   ( ) Mary's young son is in the shopping cart.

   Write: _____

4. ( ) All of the food is on the counter.

   ( ) Soup and rice are in the shopping cart.

   ( ) Judy's meat is on the counter.

   Write: _____

Exercise 3: Letter Words

Directions: Write the words with the same first letter.

	c	m
cart	*cart*	*many*
many		
cash	_____	_____
eggs		
cashier	_____	_____
on		e
cheap	_____	
meat	_____	*eggs*
checkout		
milk	_____	_____
chicken		
out	_____	o
coming	_____	
expensive		*on*
counter	_____	_____
		_____

Exercise 4: THINK

Directions: This exercise is about you. Circle the right answer.

1. My mother is here.   yes   no

2. My brother's house is big.   yes   no

3. My neighbor's house is next to my house. yes   no

4. My doctor's office is on Elm Street.   yes   no

5. My father's car is small.   yes   no

Write the yes sentences.

_____

_____

_____

_____

Lesson Seven

AT KING'S RESTAURANT

breakfast	fish	lot	reading
can	french fries	lunch	sandwich
children	hamburger	manager	small
coffee	have	medium	soda
cook	hungry	menu	tea
dinner	kitchen	or	very
eating	large	order	watching

Write:

breakfast _____   lot _____

can _____   lunch _____

children _____   manager _____

coffee _____   medium _____

cook _____   menu _____

dinner _____   or _____

eating _____   order _____

fish _____   reading _____

french fries _____   sandwich _____

hamburger _____   small _____

have _____   soda _____

hungry _____   tea _____

kitchen _____   very _____

large _____   watching _____

Phrases

a hamburger and french fries   a cook and a waiter
hungry children   coffee or tea
a large kitchen   eating dinner
two medium sodas   reading the menu
a fish sandwich   large or small
breakfast or lunch   four hamburgers

Write:

a hamburger and french fries _____

hungry children _____

a large kitchen _____

two medium sodas _____

a fish sandwich _____

breakfast or lunch _____

a cook and a waiter _____

coffee or tea _____

eating dinner _____

reading the menu _____

large or small _____

four hamburgers _____

Sentences

1. Don and Tim are eating dinner.

2. They are very hungry.

3. They're eating a lot of hamburgers and large french fries.

4. Mrs. Green is reading the menu.

5. She is going to order.

6. The cashier is watching her.

7. They have to work a lot.

8. They can work in the kitchen or behind the counter.

9. The manager is watching them.

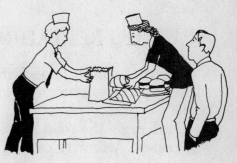

Write:

5. _____

7. _____

8. _____

MENU		SMALL	MEDIUM	LARGE
HAMBURGER .50	COFFEE	.35	.50	.75
FRENCH FRIES .45	TEA		.50	
CHICKEN SANDWICH 1.15	SODA	.40	.60	.80
FISH SANDWICH .95	MILK	.25	.45	

AT KING'S RESTAURANT

The Bond family is in King's Restaurant. They're going to eat lunch there. The children are very hungry. They have to eat now.

At King's the food is cheap. There are no waiters or waitresses. A family can buy a lot of food there. A family can eat breakfast, lunch, or dinner there.

The Bonds are reading the menu. A cook is cooking hamburgers in the kitchen. Three cashiers are behind the counter. The manager is watching the cashiers.

Mr. Bond is going to order two hamburgers, french fries, and a large coffee. Mrs. Bond is going to order a chicken sandwich and a small tea. Ben is going to order a hamburger, french fries, and milk. Bob is going to order a fish sandwich, french fries, and a medium soda.

They can eat in the restaurant or in their car. They are going to eat in the restaurant.

Exercise 1: Match and Check — Phrases and Sentences

Directions: Check (√) the right answer. Write the right answer.

1.

( )   a chicken sandwich

( )   french fries and a hamburger

( )   a medium coffee

Write: _____

2.

( )   four hungry boys

( )   watching the manager

( )   behind the police officer

Write: _____

3.

( )   The children can read the menu.

( )   The family is eating dinner.

( )   Kate is ordering food.

Write: _____

4.

( )   The manager is working in the kitchen.

( )   The cashier is working behind the counter.

( )   The people are buying their food.

Write: _____

Exercise 2: Words and Pictures

Directions: Look at the picture. Write the names of 10 things in the picture.

children	coffee	apples	waiter	police officer
french fries	cook	soda	cash	cart
hamburger	kitchen	menu	car	manager

1. _____   4. _____   8. _____

2. _____   5. _____   9. _____

3. _____   6. _____   10. _____

                       7. _____

Exercise 3: THINK

Directions: This exercise is about you. Circle the right answer.

	yes	no
1. I can write.	yes	no
2. I can type.	yes	no
3. I have to eat food.	yes	no
4. My mother can park her car.	yes	no
5. My brother has to work today.	yes	no
6. My father can cook.	yes	no
7. I have to live in America.	yes	no

Exercise 4: Read, Write, and Talk

Directions:
1. Read the menu.
2. Write your order.
3. Talk to the person next to you. Write his or her order. Write his or her name at the top of the order.

—— Menu ——

	Small	Medium	Large
HAMBURGER	.50		
FRENCH FRIES	.45		
CHICKEN SANDWICH	1.15		
FISH SANDWICH	.95		
COFFEE	.35	.50	.75
TEA	.35	.50	
SODA	.40	.60	.80
MILK	.25	.45	

MY ORDER

_____

_____

_____

_____

_____

TOTAL _____

_____'S ORDER

_____

_____

_____

_____

_____

TOTAL _____

Lesson Eight

A SALE AT SAM'S

blouse	money	size	tomorrow
clothes	new	skirt	too
coat	night	slacks	underwear
dress	price	spend	wear
for	sale	suit	with
has	shirt	sweater	women
jacket	shoe		

Write:

blouse _____

clothes _____

coat _____

dress _____

for _____

has _____

jacket _____

money _____

new _____

night _____

price _____

sale _____

shirt _____

shoe _____

size _____

skirt _____

slacks _____

spend _____

suit _____

sweater _____

tomorrow _____

too _____

underwear _____

wear _____

with _____

women _____

Phrases

his new jacket

a dress and a coat

a lot of clothes

on sale

with two women

tomorrow night

my old shirt

with her new skirt

with his new suit

his size

a cheap price

Write:

his new jacket _____

a dress and a coat _____

a lot of clothes _____

on sale _____

with two women _____

tomorrow night _____

my old shirt _____

with her new skirt _____

with his new suit _____

his size _____

a cheap price _____

Sentences

1. Pam is wearing expensive clothes.

2. She is going to spend money at the sale.

3. She has to buy new underwear.

4. Jeff is going to have dinner with his boss.

5. He has to buy new clothes.

6. He's going to buy new shoes, slacks, and two shirts.

7. Mrs. Lane is buying clothes for her children.

8. She's buying a blouse and a sweater for her daughter.

9. She's buying a sweater for her son, too.

Write:

2. _____

5. _____

8. _____

A SALE AT SAM'S

Sam's is a clothing store. There is a sale at Sam's today. Men's, women's, and children's clothes are cheap. Many people are in the store.

Men's shirts and slacks are on sale. Women's blouses, skirts, and sweaters are on sale. Children's underwear is on sale, too.

The Hill family is in the store. Mrs. Hill is shopping for a dress. She has to buy the dress today. She is going to wear it to work tomorrow. She is going to buy shoes to wear with her new dress. Her shoe size is 6.

Mr. Hill is shopping for a new suit. He is going to an expensive restaurant with his boss tomorrow night.

Mr. and Mrs. Hill have to buy clothes for their children. They have to buy a jacket for their son and a coat for their daughter. Children's coats and jackets aren't on sale today. They are expensive. The price of the coat is $23.00. The price of the jacket is $26.00.

Many people are going to buy clothes. They are going to spend a lot of money at Sam's today.

Exercise 1: Match and Check — Phrases and Sentences

Directions: Check (√) the right answer. Write the right answer.

1.

    ( )   a cheap price

    ( )   a size 7 dress

    ( )   slacks and a jacket

Write: _____

2.

    ( )   my son's underwear

    ( )   women's shoes

    ( )   two new coats

Write: _____

3.

    ( )   He is going to wear that new shirt with his suit.

    ( )   She is wearing a skirt and a blouse.

    ( )   That new coat is expensive.

Write: _____

4.

    ( )   He is buying a coat for his wife.

    ( )   They are buying sweaters for their children.

    ( )   Carmen's jacket is cheap.

Write: _____

Exercise 2:

Directions: Write the right words.

blouse	dress	skirt
shoes	sweater	coat
jacket	underwear	slacks
suit	shirt	

men's clothes   women's clothes

_____   _____

_____   _____

_____   _____

men's or women's clothes

_____   _____

_____   _____

_____   _____

_____   _____

Exercise 3: THINK

Directions: These sentences are about you. Circle the right answer.

1. I'm going to eat in a restaurant tomorrow.   yes   no
2. I'm going to shop in a supermarket tomorrow.   yes   no
3. I'm going to cook hamburgers tomorrow.   yes   no
4. I'm going to buy new clothes tomorrow.   yes   no
5. I'm going to clean my house tomorrow.   yes   no
6. I'm going to go to my doctor's office tomorrow.   yes   no
7. I'm going to look for a new apartment tomorrow.   yes   no
8. I'm going to watch TV tomorrow.   yes   no

Exercise 4:

Directions: Find the word that doesn't belong with the others. Circle that word.

EXAMPLE	A	B
one	mother	jacket
four	father	firemen
(shoes)	sister	shirt
three	cat	underwear
two	brother	suit

C	D	E
mother	telephone	husband
grandmother	cook	daughter
sister	janitor	father
wife	secretary	brother
man	nurse	son-in-law

F	G
post office	eggs
supermarket	chicken
apartment	address
fire station	milk
cashier	rice

Check-Up Lessons 5–8

Exercise 1: Match and Check

Directions: Check (✓) the right answer. Write the right answer.

1.

    ( ) behind the counter

    ( ) in the shopping cart

    ( ) in front of the store

Write: _____

2.

    ( ) french fries and a hamburger

    ( ) paying the cashier

    ( ) two hungry boys

Write: _____

3.

    ( ) going in the police station

    ( ) two firemen

    ( ) in the post office

Write: _____

4.

    ( ) They are shopping for new clothes.

    ( ) She is wearing a skirt.

    ( ) He is wearing a new jacket.

Write: _____

5.

    ( ) The cook is working in the kitchen.

    ( ) The cashier is behind the counter.

    ( ) The family is eating dinner.

Write: _____

Exercise 2: Words and Pictures

Directions: Look at the picture. Write the names of 9 things in the picture.

police officer   clothing store   shopping cart
stop sign   restaurant   firemen
post office   car   fire station
supermarket   menu   apartment building
kitchen

1. _____   2. _____   3. _____

4. _____   5. _____   6. _____

7. _____   8. _____   9. _____

Lesson Nine

do _____   insurance _____
don't _____   me _____
feel _____   occupation _____
head _____   sick _____
health _____   stomach _____
hello _____   what _____
help _____   where _____
hot _____   you _____
hurts _____   your _____

AT THE HOSPITAL

Nurse: Hello, can I help you?

Ted: Yes, I feel very sick. My stomach hurts a lot and my head is very hot.

Nurse: What is your name, address, and telephone number?

Ted: My name is Ted Briggs, my address is 312 Elm Street, and my telephone number is 267-5126.

Nurse: What's your age and date of birth?

Ted: I'm 36 and my date of birth is July 24, 1946.

Nurse: What's your occupation? Where do you work?

Ted: I'm a waiter. I work in a restaurant.

Nurse: Do you have health insurance?

Ted: No, I don't.

Nurse: Are you going to give me the money now?

Ted: Yes, I am.

Nurse: You can sit there.

1. How does Ted feel? Underline the answer.
2. What's Ted's occupation? Circle the answer.
3. Where does Ted work? Underline the answer two times.
4. Does Ted have health insurance? Underline the answer three times.

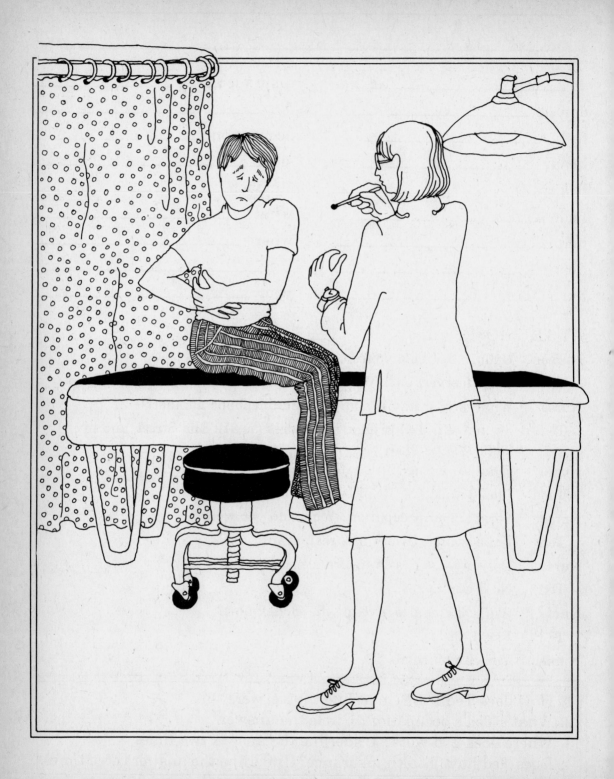

call _____	left _____
degrees _____	right _____
does _____	side _____
doesn't _____	sleep _____
high _____	take _____
hospital _____	temperature _____
how _____	whose _____

Doctor: Hello, I'm Doctor Bell and I work here at Cedars Hospital. What's your name?

Ted: My name is Ted Briggs.

Doctor: Your temperature is very high. It's 103 degrees. How are you feeling?

Ted: My stomach hurts a lot and I feel very hot.

Doctor: Does your head hurt?

Ted: No, it doesn't.

Doctor: Does your stomach hurt on the left side or the right side?

Ted: On the right side.

Doctor: You are very sick. You're going to take this medicine and sleep at the hospital.

Ted: OK. I have to call my wife.

Doctor: You can call on the nurse's telephone.

---

5. Where does the doctor work? Underline the answer.
6. Does Ted's head hurt? Circle the answer.
7. Does Ted's stomach hurt on the left side or the right side? Underline the answer two times.
8. Where is Ted going to sleep? Underline the answer three times.
9. Whose telephone can Ted call on? Circle the answer two times.

Exercise 1: Match the Sound

Directions: Write the words that have the same sound as the letter underlined.

you	it's	sick	sister	this
I	high	right	side	new
sit	yes	your	in	name
number	next	neighbor	is	

<u>n</u>o   b<u>i</u>g   <u>y</u>oung   ri<u>c</u>e

name _____ _____ _____

_____ _____ _____ _____

_____ _____ _____ _____

_____ _____ _____ _____

_____ _____

_____

_____

Exercise 2: Match-Ups

Directions: Draw a line from the question to the right answer.

1. What is your name?   A. My stomach hurts a lot.

2. What is your age?   B. My name is Ted Briggs.

3. What is your date of birth?   C. I'm 36 years old.

4. What's your occupation?   D. My birth date is July 24, 1946.

5. How are you feeling?   E. I'm a waiter.

Exercise 3: Word Study

A. Directions: Study the words and the picture. Write the words.

head _____

eyes _____

nose _____

mouth _____

neck _____

shoulder _____

arm _____

stomach _____

hand _____

finger _____

leg _____

foot _____

toe _____

B. Directions: Study the picture. Write the right word.

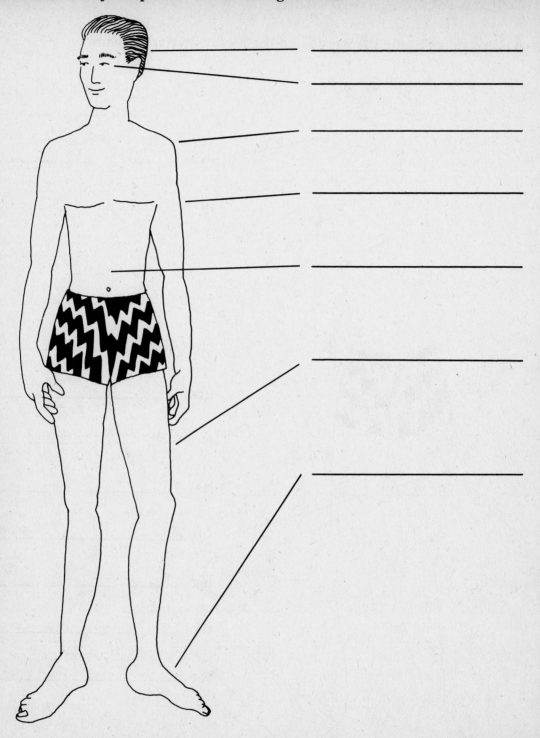

Exercise 4: THINK

A. Directions: Look at the picture. Write the right word.

Dot's _____ hurts.

Tom's _____ hurts.

Lynn's _____ hurts.

Bella's _____ hurts.

Bud's _____ hurts.

Al's _____ hurts.

B. Directions: Look at the pictures. Write the right answer.

1. Whose arm hurts? _____ .

2. Whose neck hurts? _____ .

3. Whose foot hurts? _____ .

4. Whose head hurts? _____ .

5. Whose stomach hurts? _____ .

6. Whose finger hurts? _____ .

another	_____	much	_____
appointment	_____	pay	_____
information	_____	use	_____
make	_____	want	_____

RENTING AN APARTMENT

Pat: I want to rent another apartment. My apartment is small. It has one bedroom and a small kitchen. I want an apartment with two bedrooms, a kitchen, and a large living room.

Carol: How much rent can you pay?

Pat: I can pay $300 a month.

Carol: There's an apartment for rent on this street.

Pat: There's a FOR RENT sign and a telephone number to call for more information.

Carol: That's a new building. Where can you park your car?

Pat: There is a parking lot behind the building.

Carol: There's a telephone. You can use it to make an appointment.

---

1. What does Pat want to rent? Underline the answer.
2. Why? Circle the answer.
3. How much rent can Pat pay? Underline the answer two times.
4. Where is the parking lot? Underline the answer three times.

bathroom _____ include _____

but _____ meet _____

day _____ month _____

eight _____ o'clock _____

every _____ room _____

good _____ see _____

heat _____ water _____

Pat: Hello, do you have an apartment for rent at 19 Elm Street?

Landlord: Yes, I do.

Pat: How many rooms does it have?

Landlord: It has two bedrooms, a living room, a kitchen, and a bathroom.

Pat: What's the rent?

Landlord: The rent is $275 a month.

Pat: Does the rent include heat and hot water?

Landlord: Yes, it does.

Pat: Oh, that's good. I want to make an appointment to see it.

Landlord: Can you meet me there tomorrow at one o'clock?

Pat: No, I work every day. But I can come at night.

Landlord: Can you come at eight o'clock?

Pat: Yes. I'll see you tomorrow night.

5. How many rooms does the apartment have? Underline the answer.
6. What's the rent? Circle the answer.
7. Does the rent include heat and hot water? Underline the answer two times.
8. When does Pat work? Underline the answer three times.
9. When can Pat see the apartment? Underline the answer four times.

Exercise 1: Match the Sound

Directions: Write the words that have the same sound as the letter underlined.

rent	can	has	soda	sale
cash	that	month	apple	date
meet	above	pay	read	rice
a	take	much	at	slacks
day				

c<u>a</u>t   m<u>a</u>n   <u>r</u>estaurant   n<u>a</u>me

cash   _____   _____   _____

_____   _____   _____   _____

_____   _____   _____   _____

_____   <u>a</u>cross

_____   _____   _____

_____   _____   _____

_____   _____

_____   _____

Exercise 2: Match-Ups

Directions: Draw a line from the question to the right answer.

1. How much rent can you pay?

2. Where can I park?

3. How much is it?

4. How many rooms does the apartment have?

5. Can you come at 8:00?

A. It has four rooms.

B. There is a parking lot behind the building.

C. I can pay $300 a month.

D. The rent is $275 a month.

E. Yes, I can.

Exercise 3: Word Study

A. Directions: Study the words and picture. Write the words.

1 one	4 four	7 seven	10 ten
2 two	5 five	8 eight	11 eleven
3 three	6 six	9 nine	12 twelve

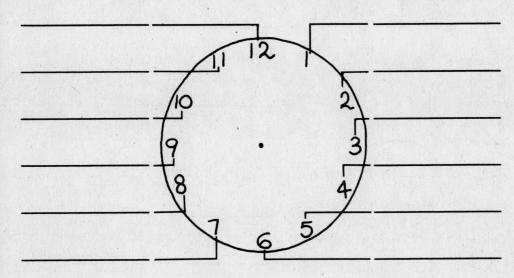

B. Directions:

Read:

1. twelve o'clock
2. noon
3. twelve noon
4. twelve o'clock
5. midnight
6. twelve midnight

Write:

1. *twelve o'clock*
2. _____
3. _____
4. _____
5. _____
6. _____

C. Directions: Look at the picture. Write the right word or number.

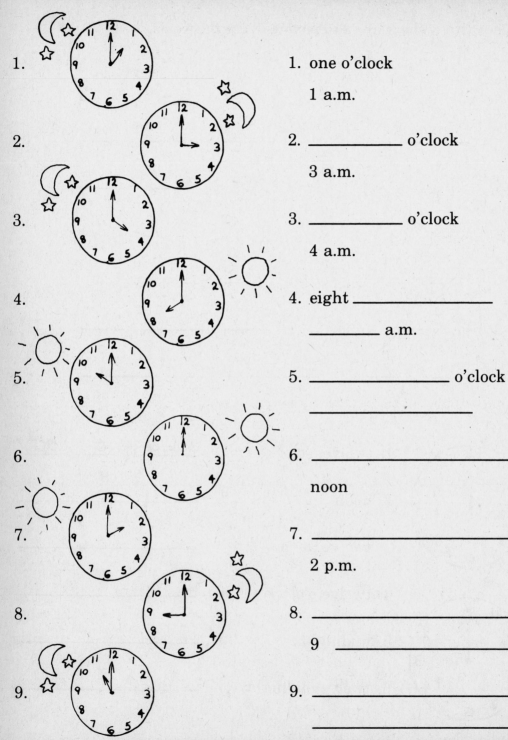

1. one o'clock

   1 a.m.

2. _____ o'clock

   3 a.m.

3. _____ o'clock

   4 a.m.

4. eight _____

   _____ a.m.

5. _____ o'clock

   _____

6. _____

   noon

7. _____

   2 p.m.

8. _____

   9 _____

9. _____

   _____

Exercise 4: THINK

Directions: This exercise is about you. Write *Yes, I do* or *No, I don't* after each question.

1. Do you live with your parents? _____

2. Do you live in an apartment? _____

3. Do you have a landlord? _____

4. Do you work in an office building? _____

5. Do you wear expensive clothes? _____

6. Do you eat breakfast every day? _____

7. Do you cook dinner every day? _____

8. Do you have health insurance? _____

9. Do you work in a restaurant? _____

10. Do you have a new coat? _____

11. Do you call your boss on the telephone? _____

12. Do you park behind your building? _____

Lesson Eleven

ahead _____   long _____

begin _____   minutes _____

blocks _____   right _____

bus _____   straight _____

classes _____   thank _____

directions _____ then _____

excuse _____   traffic light _____

give _____   Tuesday _____

left _____   walk _____

ASKING FOR DIRECTIONS

Marco: Excuse me, Mr. Kelly, I have to go to Bristol College. Can you give me directions?

Mr. Kelly: Yes, I can. First you walk three blocks to the bus stop and then you take bus 93.

Marco: Can you give me directions to the bus stop?

Mr. Kelly: OK. Walk straight ahead one block on Second Street to Elm Street, take a left on Elm and walk one block. Take a right on Fourth Street and walk one block to the traffic light. That's Bond Street. The bus stop is on the corner of Bond Street and Fourth Street.

Marco: Thank you. How long is it going to take to walk to the bus stop?

Mr. Kelly: It's going to take ten minutes.

Marco: That's OK. Classes begin at seven o'clock every Tuesday.

---

1. Where does Marco have to go? Underline the answer.
2. What does Marco have to do first? Circle the answer.
3. Where is the bus stop? Underline the answer two times.
4. How long is it going to take to walk to the bus stop? Underline the answer three times.
5. At what time do classes begin? Underline the answer four times.

cents _____   fifty _____

change _____   please _____

dollar _____   speak _____

driver _____   slowly _____

English _____   understand _____

exact _____   well _____

fare _____

Marco:	Excuse me. I want to go to Bristol College on Main Street. Is this the right bus?
Bus Driver:	Yes, this is bus 93.
Marco:	What's the fare?
Bus Driver:	Fifty cents.
Marco:	Here's a dollar.
Bus Driver:	No, you have to give me the exact fare.
Marco:	Excuse me. I don't speak English very well. I don't understand. Please speak slowly.
Bus Driver:	Give me fifty cents. I can't give you change.
Marco:	OK, here's fifty cents.
Bus Driver:	Go ahead and sit there.

6. On what street is Bristol College? Underline the answer.
7. What is the right bus? Circle the answer.
8. What's the fare? Underline the answer two times.

Exercise 1: Match the Sound

Directions: Write the words that have the same sound as the letter underlined.

fare	excuse	street	three
yes	landlord	exact	begin
lunch	when	then	directions
cents	father	liquor	four
	speak	me	

desk   live   he   feel

_____ _____ _____ _____

_____ _____ _____ _____

_____ _____ _____ _____

_____ _____ _____

_____ _____

_____

Exercise 2: Match-Ups

Directions: Draw a line from the question to the right answer.

1. How long is it going to take to walk to the bus stop?

   A. It's on the corner of Bond Street and Fourth Street.

2. Can you give me directions?

   B. Yes, I can.

3. Is this bus 93?

   C. Yes, it is.

4. What's the fare?

   D. Fifty cents.

5. Where is the bus stop?

   E. It's going to take 10 minutes.

Exercise 3: Word Study

BRENDA'S CALENDAR FOR JUNE

SUNDAY	MONDAY	TUESDAY	WEDNESDAY	THURSDAY	FRIDAY	SATURDAY
	1 *Pay the rent*	**2** *Go to class*	**3** *Go to Dr. Bell's*	**4** *Call mother*	**5** *Go shopping*	**6** *Clean house*
7	**8**	**9** *Go to class*	**10**	**11**	**12** *Go shopping*	**13** *Clean house*
14	**15**	**16** *Go to class*	**17**	**18**	**19** *Go shopping*	**20** *Clean house*
21	**22**	**23** *Go to class*	**24**	**25**	**26** *Go shopping*	**27** *Clean house*
28	**29**	**30** *Go to class*				

A. Directions: Look at the calendar. Write the days of the week.

Sunday _____   _____

_____   _____

_____   _____

_____

B. Directions: Look at the calendar. Circle the right answer.

1. Is Brenda going to pay the rent on Monday, June 1?   yes   no

2. Does Brenda go to class every Wednesday?   yes   no

3. Is Brenda going to go to Dr. Bell's office on
    Tuesday, June 9?   yes   no

4. Is Brenda going to call her mother on Thursday,
    June 4?   yes   no

5. Does Brenda clean her house every Saturday?   yes   no

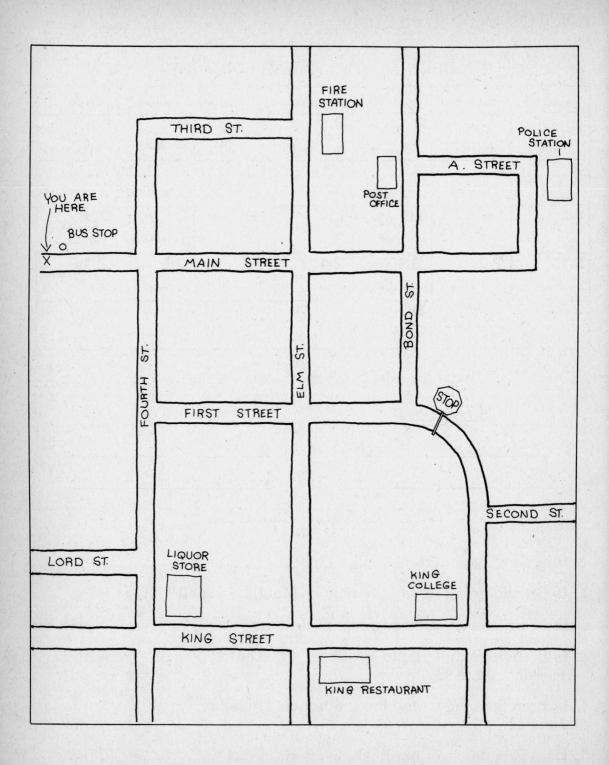

Exercise 4: THINK

Directions: Look at the map on page 94. Then read the directions below and answer the questions. Start at the bus stop for every question.

1. Walk straight ahead two blocks. Take a left and walk one block.

   Where are you? _____

2. Walk straight ahead two blocks. Take a right and walk two blocks. Take a left and walk one block.

   Where are you? _____

3. Walk straight ahead one block. Take a right and walk three blocks. Take a left and walk one block.

   Where are you? _____

4. Walk straight ahead three blocks. Take a left and walk one block. Take a right and walk one block.

   Where are you? _____

5. Walk two blocks straight ahead to Elm Street. Take a right at Elm. Walk one block to First Street. Take a left on First Street and walk to the stop sign. Take a left at the stop sign. That's Bond Street. Walk straight ahead on Bond Street for two blocks.

   Where are you? _____

6. Walk straight ahead three blocks. Take a right and walk one block. Take another right and walk one block. Take another right and walk one block. Take a left and walk two blocks.

   Where are you? _____

Check-Up Lessons 9–11

Exercise 1: Match and Check

Directions: Write the right word.

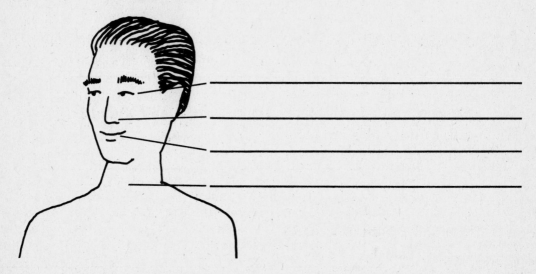

_____

_____

_____

_____

Exercise 2:

Directions: Look at the clock. Write the right words.

1.

_____ o'clock

10:00 _____

2.

_____

_____

3.

_____

_____

Exercise 3:

Directions: Write the missing days of the week.

Sunday _____

_____ _____

_____ *Saturday*

Wednesday

Exercise 4: Letter Words

Directions: Write the words that have the same sound as the letter
underlined.

see	with	sleep
him	help	then
day	eight	include
please	milk	they

she_   f_ish   we__l   _make

_____   _____   _____   _____

_____   _____   _____   _____

_____   _____   _____   _____

_____

Lesson Twelve

AT THE PHARMACY

Pharmacist:	Can I help you?
Mr. Todd:	I have two prescriptions. Can you fill them?
Pharmacist:	Yes, but you have to wait a few minutes.
Mr. Todd:	OK.
Pharmacist:	Mr. Todd, here is your medicine. It's in two bottles.
Mr. Todd:	Two bottles?
Pharmacist:	Yes. This is your first prescription. It is in a big bottle. You have to take two tablets three times a day. Take two tablets in the morning, two in the afternoon, and two at bedtime.
Mr. Todd:	Can I drive after I take this medicine?
Pharmacist:	No, you can't.
Mr. Todd:	Why?
Pharmacist:	It's going to make you sleepy.
Mr. Todd:	Can you refill this prescription?
Pharmacist:	No, I can't. First you have to see your doctor.
Mr. Todd:	I understand.
Pharmacist:	Your second prescription is different. It's in a small bottle. Take it two or three hours after lunch.
Mr. Todd:	Why?
Pharmacist:	You have to take this medicine when your stomach is empty.
Mr. Todd:	Thank you. How much are they?
Pharmacist:	$18.56. Thank you.

after _____		morning _____	
afternoon _____		pharmacy _____	
bedtime _____		prescriptions _____	
bottles _____		sleepy _____	
can't _____		tablets _____	
drive _____		times _____	
few _____		wait _____	
fill _____		why _____	

Pharmacist: Can I help you?

Mr. Todd: I have two prescriptions. Can you fill them?

Pharmacist: Yes, but you have to wait a few minutes.

Mr. Todd: OK.

Pharmacist: Mr. Todd, here is your medicine. It's in two bottles.

Mr. Todd: Two bottles?

Pharmacist: Yes. This is your first prescription. It is in a big bottle. You have to take two tablets three times a day. Take two tablets in the morning, two in the afternoon, and two at bedtime.

Mr. Todd: Can I drive after I take this medicine?

Pharmacist: No, you can't.

Mr. Todd: Why?

Pharmacist: It's going to make you sleepy.

---

1. How many prescriptions does Mr. Todd have? Underline the answer.
2. How many bottles is it in? Circle the answer.
3. How many times a day does Mr. Todd have to take his first prescription? Underline the answer two times.
4. Is this medicine going to make Mr. Todd sleepy?   yes   no

different _____	refill _____
empty _____	these _____
pharmacist _____	when _____

Mr. Todd: Can you refill this prescription?

Pharmacist: No, I can't. First you have to see your doctor.

Mr. Todd: I understand.

Pharmacist: Your second prescription is different. It's in a small bottle. Take one of these tablets every day. Take it two or three hours after lunch.

Mr. Todd: Why?

Pharmacist: You have to take this medicine when your stomach is empty.

Mr. Todd: Thank you. How much are they?

Pharmacist: $18.56. Thank you.

---

5. Can the pharmacist refill this prescription? yes   no
6. Does Mr. Todd have to take the second prescription when his stomach is empty? yes   no
7. How much are they? _____

Exercise 1: Match the Sound

Directions: Write the words that have the same sound as the letter
or letters underlined.

two	hospital	son
hello	telephone	mother
lot	doctor	don't
going	stomach	hot
	do	to

bottle   t<u>oo</u>   n<u>o</u>   <u>o</u>f

_____ _____ _____ _____

_____ _____ _____ _____

_____ _____ _____ _____

_____ _____

Exercise 2: Match-Ups

Directions: Draw a line from the question to the right answer.

1. Can you refill this prescription?

2. Can I drive after I take this medicine?

3. Can I help you?

4. How many prescriptions do you have?

A. No, you can't.

B. I have two.

C. No, I can't.

D. Yes, I want to pay for this medicine.

Exercise 3: Word Study

A. Directions: Study the words and the picture. Write the words.

name of pharmacist	**ACE PHARMACY**	name of pharmacy
	Ed Brook R.Ph.	
prescription number	No.135125 Date 1/25/82	date prescription filled
patient's name	John Reed	
name of medicine	Take 1 tablet 4 times daily.	dosage
name of doctor	Ornade	
	Dane	

```
              ACE PHARMACY
          Ed Brook R.Ph.

       No.135125          Date 1/25/82
       John Reed
          Take 1 tablet 4 times daily.
       Ornade
       Dane
```

_____   _____

_____   _____

_____   _____

_____

_____

B. Directions: Answer the questions.

1. What is the pharmacist's name? _____

2. What is the prescription number? _____

3. What is the dosage? _____

4. Is John going to take this medicine every day? _____

5. What is the name of the medicine? _____

C. Directions: Answer the questions.

KING'S PHARMACY

Ann Parr R. Ph.

No. 23604   Date 2/6/82

Jean Hall

      Take 2 tablets at bedtime.

Penicillin

Wolf

1. What is the pharmacist's name? _____

2. What is the prescription number? _____

3. What is the dosage? _____

4. Is Jean going to take this medicine in the morning? _____

5. What is the name of the medicine? _____

D. Directions: Read the directions. Look at the picture. Write the directions.

1. _____*Take with food or milk.*_____

Take with food or milk.

2. _____

This prescription cannot be refilled.

3. _____

Take on an empty stomach.

4. _____

Will cause drowsiness.

5. _____

Use care when operating a car.

6. _____

_____

WARNING! Keep this and other medications out of reach of children.

Exercise 4: THINK

Directions: Look at the picture. Write the right answer.

Example: *Use care when operating a car*.

1. _____

2. _____

3. _____

4. _____

5. _____

Lesson Thirteen

13

REGISTERING FOR A CLASS

Jan: We want to register for night classes. I want to take typing and my friend Elena wants to learn English. She lived in Puerto Rico for nineteen years. She came to America in October. She doesn't speak English.

Secretary: Our typing class starts next week on Monday, January 11, at 6:30 p.m. It's a two-hour class and costs $65.00. The class is eight weeks long. The semester ends on Monday, March 1. Is that OK?

Jan: Yes, that's good.

Secretary: I'm going to ask you questions and fill out the registration form. What are your first, middle, and last names?

Jan: My first name is Jan, my middle name is Anna, and my last name is Blair.

Secretary: What is your address, telephone number, and social security number?

Jan: My address is 26 Elm Street and my telephone number is 235-1872. My social security number is 142-90-6378.

Secretary: When were you born?

Jan: My birth date is June 15, 1948.

Secretary: OK. Now, your friend's English class started last week, on Tuesday, December 30.

Jan: When is the next class?

Secretary: It's tomorrow, Tuesday, January 5, at 6:15 p.m. The class is ten weeks long. The semester ends on Tuesday, March 2. It's a three-hour class and costs $75.00.

Jan: That's fine.

Secretary: Give me your friend's name, address, and telephone number.

Jan: Her first name is Elena, her middle name is Maria, and her last name is Mora. Her address is 24 Elm Street, and her telephone number is 235-1732.

Secretary: When was she born? Where was she born?

Jan: Her birth date is May 29, 1947. She was born in Puerto Rico.

Secretary: Did she attend school in Puerto Rico?

Jan: Yes, she attended school for ten years.

Secretary: Thank you. You can pay next week. Good luck in your classes.

ask _____		nineteen _____	
came _____		questions _____	
costs _____		register _____	
ends _____		registration _____	
form _____		security _____	
friend _____		semester _____	
hour _____		social _____	
last _____		starts _____	
learn _____		week _____	
middle _____		year _____	

Jan: We want to register for night classes. I want to take typing and my friend Elena wants to learn English. She lived in Puerto Rico for nineteen years. She came to America in October. She doesn't speak English.

Secretary: Our typing class starts next week on Monday, January 11, at 6:30 p.m. It's a two-hour class and costs $65.00. The class is eight weeks long. The semester ends on Monday, March 1. Is that OK?

Jan: Yes, that's good.

Secretary: I'm going to ask you questions and fill out the registration form. What are your first, middle, and last names?

Jan: My first name is Jan, my middle name is Anna, and my last name is Blair.

Secretary: What is your address, telephone number, and social security number?

Jan: My address is 26 Elm Street and my telephone number is 235-1872. My social security number is 142-90-6378.

---

1. What class does Jan want to take? Underline the answer.
2. What does Elena want to learn? Circle the answer.
3. How long does the typing class last? Underline the answer two times.

attend _____	luck _____
born _____	school _____
did _____	was _____
fine _____	were _____

Secretary: When were you born?

Jan: My birth date is June 15, 1948.

Secretary: OK. Now, your friend's English class started last week, on Tuesday, December 30.

Jan: When is the next class?

Secretary: It's tomorrow, Tuesday, January 5, at 6:15 p.m. The class is ten weeks long. The semester ends on Tuesday, March 2. It's a three-hour class and costs $75.00.

Jan: That's fine.

Secretary: Give me your friend's name, address, and telephone number.

Jan: Her first name is Elena, her middle name is Maria, and her last name is Mora. Her address is 24 Elm Street, and her telephone number is 235-1732.

Secretary: When was she born? Where was she born?

Jan: Her birth date is May 29, 1947. She was born in Puerto Rico.

Secretary: Did she attend school in Puerto Rico?

Jan: Yes, she attended school for ten years.

Secretary: Thank you. You can pay next week. Good luck in your classes.

---

4. What is Jan's birth date? _____
5. How much does the English class cost? _____
6. When was Elena born? _____
7. Did Elena attend school in Puerto Rico?   yes   no
8. Can Elena and Jan pay next week?   yes   no

Exercise 1: Match the Sound

Directions: Write the words that have the same sound as the letter underlined.

bedtime	big	born
costs	can't	came
did	birth	dollar
coffee	different	bottles

_bus   _can   _desk

_____   _____   _____

_____   _____   _____

_____   _____   _____

_____   _____

_____

Exercise 2: Match-Ups

Directions: Draw a line from the question to the right answer.

1. What are your first, middle, and last names?

2. What is your address?

3. What is your friend's name?

4. When is the next class?

A. My address is 26 Elm Street.

B. My first name is Jan, my middle name is Anna, and my last name is Blair.

C. It's tomorrow at 6:15 p.m.

D. Her name is Elena Maria Mora.

Exercise 3: Word Study

A. Directions: Look at the picture. Write the names of the months.

1982
CALENDAR

JANUARY								FEBRUARY								MARCH					
SUN	MON	TUE	WED	THU	FRI	SAT		SUN	MON	TUE	WED	THU	FRI	SAT		SUN	MON	TUE	WED	THU	FRI	SAT

JANUARY

SUN MON TUE WED THU FRI SAT

					1	2
3	4	5	6	7	8	9
10	(11)	12	13	14	15	16
17	18	19	20	21	22	23
24	25	26	27	28	29	30
31

FEBRUARY

SUN MON TUE WED THU FRI SAT

	1	2	3	4	5	6
7	8	9	10	11	12	13
14	15	16	17	18	19	20
21	22	23	24	25	26	27
28

MARCH

SUN MON TUE WED THU FRI SAT

	1	2	3	4	5	6
7	8	9	10	11	12	13
14	15	16	17	18	19	20
21	22	23	24	25	26	27
28	29	30	31

APRIL

				1	2	3
4	5	6	7	8	9	10
11	12	13	14	15	16	17
18	19	20	21	(22)	23	24
25	26	27	28	29	30

MAY

						1
2	3	4	5	6	7	8
9	10	11	12	13	14	15
16	17	18	19	20	21	22
23	24	25	26	27	28	29
30	31

JUNE

		1	2	(3)	4	5
6	7	8	9	10	11	12
13	14	15	16	17	18	19
20	21	22	23	24	25	26
27	28	29	30

JULY

				1	2	3
4	5	6	7	8	9	10
11	12	13	14	15	16	17
18	19	20	21	22	23	24
25	26	27	28	29	30	31

AUGUST

1	2	3	4	5	6	(7)
8	9	10	11	12	13	(14)
15	16	17	18	19	20	21
22	23	24	25	26	27	28
29	30	31

SEPTEMBER

			1	2	3	4
5	6	7	8	9	10	11
12	13	14	15	16	17	18
19	20	21	22	23	24	25
26	27	28	29	30

OCTOBER

					1	2
3	4	5	6	7	8	9
10	11	12	13	14	15	16
17	18	19	20	21	22	23
24	25	26	27	28	29	30
31

NOVEMBER

	1	2	3	4	5	6
7	8	9	10	11	12	13
14	15	16	17	18	19	20
21	22	23	(24)	25	26	27
28	29	30

DECEMBER

			1	2	3	4
5	6	(7)	8	9	10	11
12	13	14	15	16	17	18
19	20	21	22	23	24	25
26	27	28	29	30	31

1. *January*

2. _____

3. _____

4. _____

5. _____

6. _____

7. _____

8. _____

9. _____

10. _____

11. _____

12. _____

111

B. Directions: What months have 31 days? Look at the calendar. Write
   the words.

_____

_____

_____

_____

_____

_____

_____

C. Directions: Look at the calendar. Write the dates that are circled.

Example: _____ *January 11, 1982* _____ | _____ *1/11/82* _____

1. _____ | _____

2. _____ | _____

3. _____ | _____

4. _____ | _____

5. _____ | _____

Exercise 4: THINK

Directions: Fill in this registration form for Jan. Use the information from the dialogue.

DIVISION OF CONTINUING EDUCATION
PLEASE PRINT CLEARLY AND BEAR DOWN WITH BALL POINT PEN

SOCIAL SECURITY NUMBER		DATE	MONTH	DAY	YEAR

LAST NAME	FIRST NAME	MIDDLE NAME

STREET NAME AND NUMBER

CITY	STATE	ZIP

PHONE NUMBER		DATE OF BIRTH MONTH DAY YEAR

Sex
☐ M–Male
   F–Female

CONTINUING EDUCATION STATUS   Date
Have you previously attended continuing education classes?   Yes–Y   No–N ☐

COURSE REGISTRATIONS

TITLE	DAY	TIME

OFFICE USE ONLY

	FIRST PAYMENT	SECOND PAYMENT
TUITION		
REGISTRATION		
LATE FEE		
OTHER		
TOTAL		
RECEIPT NO.		

FINANCIAL AID

TYPE	AMOUNT
AUTHORIZATION	

Lesson Fourteen

AT THE UNEMPLOYMENT OFFICE

Mr. Stone:	Can I help you?
Lil Costa:	Yes. I lost my job. I want to apply for unemployment.
Mr. Stone:	When did you lose your job?
Lil Costa:	Last week.
Mr. Stone:	What is your name, address, and telephone number?
Lil Costa:	My name is Lil Costa, my address is 37 Second Street, and my telephone number is 253-3893.
Mr. Stone:	What is your social security number?
Lil Costa:	279-42-1922.
Mr. Stone:	Who were your former employers?
Lil Costa:	I worked at Brook's Restaurant from January to March. Then I worked at King's Restaurant from March to last week.
Mr. Stone:	What was your job?
Lil Costa:	I was a waitress.
Mr. Stone:	Now I have to fill out this form. There are five questions. I'm going to ask the questions. Please answer yes or no.
Lil Costa:	OK.
Mr. Stone:	Did you work last week?
Lil Costa:	No.
Mr. Stone:	Did you look for work last week?
Lil Costa:	Yes.
Mr. Stone:	Did you refuse work last week?
Lil Costa:	No.
Mr. Stone:	Were you able to accept full-time work last week?
Lil Costa:	Yes.
Mr. Stone:	Did you change your address?
Lil Costa:	No.
Mr. Stone:	Good. Come here in two weeks on Wednesday, May 24, at 9 a.m. Then you can get your first unemployment check.

apply _____	lose _____
employers _____	lost _____
former _____	unemployment _____
job _____	who _____

Mr. Stone: Can I help you?

Lil Costa: Yes. I lost my job. I want to apply for unemployment.

Mr. Stone: When did you lose your job?

Lil Costa: Last week.

Mr. Stone: What is your name, address, and telephone number?

Lil Costa: My name is Lil Costa, my address is 37 Second Street, and my telephone number is 253-3893.

Mr. Stone: What is your social security number?

Lil Costa: 279-42-1922.

Mr. Stone: Who were your former employers?

Lil Costa: I worked at Brook's Restaurant from January to March. Then I worked at King's Restaurant from March to last week.

Mr. Stone: What was your job?

Lil Costa: I was a waitress.

---

1. When did Lil lose her job? Underline the answer.
2. What is Lil's address? Circle the answer.
3. Who were Lil's former employers? Write their names. _____

   _____

4. What was Lil's job? Underline the answer two times.

able _____   full-time _____

accept _____   get _____

answer _____   look _____

check _____   refuse _____

Mr. Stone: Now I have to fill out this form. There are five questions. I'm going to ask the questions. Please answer yes or no.

Lil Costa: OK.

Mr. Stone: Did you work last week?

Lil Costa: No.

Mr. Stone: Did you look for work last week?

Lil Costa: Yes.

Mr. Stone: Did you refuse work last week?

Lil Costa: No.

Mr. Stone: Were you able to accept full-time work last week?

Lil Costa: Yes.

Mr. Stone: Did you change your address?

Lil Costa: No.

Mr. Stone: Good. Come here in two weeks on Wednesday, May 24, at 9 a.m. Then you can get your first unemployment check.

---

5. How many questions is Mr. Stone going to ask? Underline the answer.
6. Did Lil work last week? yes   no
7. Was she able to accept full-time work last week? yes   no
8. Will Lil get her first check in two weeks? yes   no

117

Exercise 1: Match the Sound

Directions: Write the words that have the same sound as the letter underlined.

much	unemployment	waitress	work
occupation	job	Wednesday	excuse
week	were	number	understand
janitor	supermarket	jacket	

w̲ife	lu̲nch	u̲se	J̲anuary
_____	_____	_____	_____
_____	_____	_____	_____
_____	_____	_____	_____
_____	_____		
_____			

Exercise 2: Match-Ups

Directions: Draw a line from the question to the right answer.

1. Did you work last week?   A. I lost my job last week.

2. Who were your former employers?   B. No, I didn't.

3. When did you lose your job?   C. I was a waitress.

4. What was your job?   D. I worked at Brook's Restaurant and King's Restaurant.

Exercise 3: Word Study

Directions: Write the right time.

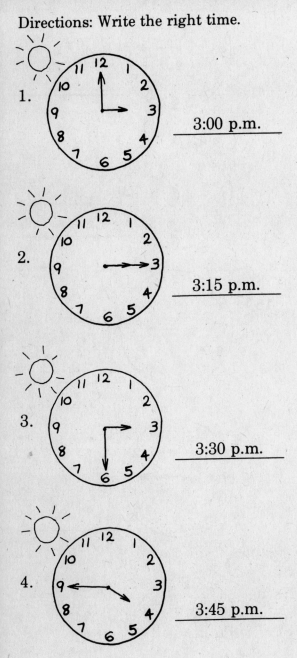

1. _____ 3:00 p.m.

2. _____ 3:15 p.m.

3. _____ 3:30 p.m.

4. _____ 3:45 p.m.

5. _____ p.m.

6. _____ 4:15

7. _____ 4:30

8. _____ 4:45

9.  _____

14.  _____

10.  _____ p.m.

15. 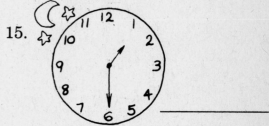 _____

11. 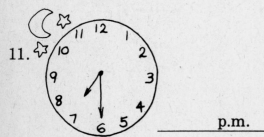 _____ p.m.

16.  _____

12. 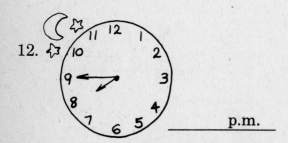 _____ p.m.

17. 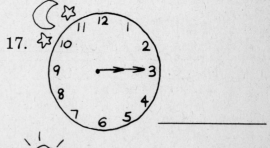 _____

13. 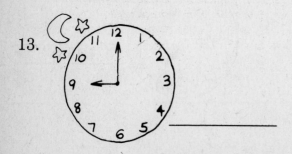 _____

18. 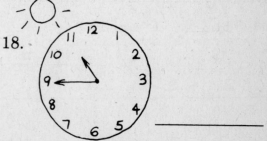 _____

120

Exercise 4: THINK

Directions: You are in an unemployment office. Fill out the form.

DIVISION OF EMPLOYMENT SECURITY
WEEKLY BENEFIT STATEMENT

WARNING

ANSWER ALL QUESTIONS CAREFULLY
CLAIMS ARE INVESTIGATED.
FALSE STATEMENTS CAN BRING
A FINE OR JAIL OR BOTH.

SOCIAL SECURITY ACCOUNT NUMBER

☐☐☐ — ☐☐ — ☐☐☐☐

DO NOT WRITE IN THIS BLOCK

Answer all questions below and present to Claims Taker
when you report.

1. Did you work last week?   Yes ☐   No ☐

2. Did you look for work last week?   Yes ☐   No ☐

3. Did you refuse work last week?   Yes ☐   No ☐

4. Were you able to accept full-time
   work last week?   Yes ☐   No ☐

5. Did you change your address?   Yes ☐   No ☐

The above answers are given under penalties of perjury.

Signature _____

PAYING BILLS

Helen: We have a lot of bills.

Paul: I know.

Helen: The telephone bill and the gas bill came in the mail today, too.

Paul: How much is the telephone bill?

Helen: $49.52.

Paul: Last month it was only $24.00. Why is it so expensive this month?

Helen: I called my sister in California and you talked to your parents in New York.

Paul: Everything is very expensive. We owe $150.00 for the rent, $23.52 for the gas bill, $49.52 for the telephone bill, $75.00 to Sam's Clothing Store, and $53.50 for the electric bill.

Helen: I paid the bill for Sam's.

Paul: I went shopping this morning at Sam's and I bought a new coat.

Helen: Oh no! There will be another bill from Sam's next month!

Paul: I know, but I needed the coat. It was cheap.

Helen: I wrote a check at the gas station this week. My car needed gas and I didn't have enough cash.

Paul: We don't have enough money to pay all of our bills. We will pay the electric bill next month.

Helen: Next month is April. We have to pay our taxes on April 15.

Paul: I think we have to take money out of our savings account. I'll go to the bank tomorrow.

Helen: Last year we saved $500.00. We're not going to save anything this year.

bills_____   mail _____

electric_____   only _____

everything _____   owe_____

gas _____

Helen: We have a lot of bills.

  Paul: I know.

Helen: The telephone bill and the gas bill came in the mail today, too.

  Paul: How much is the telephone bill?

Helen: $49.52.

  Paul: Last month it was only $24.00. Why is it so expensive this month?

Helen: I called my sister in California and you talked to your parents in New York.

  Paul: Everything is very expensive. We owe $150.00 for the rent, $23.52 for the gas bill, $49.52 for the telephone bill, $75.00 to Sam's Clothing Store, and $53.50 for the electric bill.

---

1. Which bills came in the mail? Underline the answers.
2. Is the telephone bill expensive this month? yes   no
3. How much was the telephone bill last month? Circle the answer.
4. Who called her sister? Write her name. _____
5. How much do they owe for the rent? Underline the answer two times.

account ———————	paid ————————————
all————————————	save ————————————
anything —————————	savings —————————
bank ————————————	taxes————————————
bought ———————————	think ————————————
enough——————————	went ————————————
know ————————————	will————————————
need —————————————	wrote ————————————

Helen: I paid the bill for Sam's.

Paul: I went shopping this morning at Sam's and I bought a new coat.

Helen: Oh no! There will be another bill from Sam's next month!

Paul: I know, but I needed the coat. It was cheap.

Helen: I wrote a check at the gas station this week. My car needed gas and I didn't have enough cash.

Paul: We don't have enough money to pay all of our bills. We will pay the electric bill next month.

Helen: Next month is April. We have to pay our taxes on April 15.

Paul: I think we have to take money out of our savings account. I'll go to the bank tomorrow.

Helen: Last year we saved $500.00. We're not going to save anything this year.

---

6. What did Paul buy at Sam's? Underline the answer.
7. Do they have enough money to pay all of their bills? yes   no
8. What do they have to pay in April? Write the answer. ————
9. Are they going to save any money this year? yes   no

Exercise 1: Match the Sound

Directions: Write the words that have the same sound as the letter underlined.

taxes	parking	people	pound
paid	give	Tuesday	take
gas	times	going	police
tablets	good		

<u>g</u>ood   <u>p</u>ay   <u>t</u>ea

_____ _____ _____

_____ _____ _____

_____ _____ _____

_____ _____ _____

_____ _____ _____

              _____ _____

Exercise 2: Match-Ups

Directions: Draw a line from the question to the right answer.

1. Why was the telephone bill so expensive this month?

    A. It is $49.52.

2. How much is the telephone bill?

    B. I called my sister in California.

3. Did you write any checks?

    C. Yes, we have a little.

4. Do we have money in the bank?

    D. Yes, I wrote one at the gas station.

Exercise 3: Word Study

Directions: Write the right answer. Look at the example.

Example:

 $ .25
25¢

 $1.25

1.   _____

2. _____
_____

3.    _____

4.   _____

127

5. _____

6. _____

   _____

   _____

7. _____

   _____

8. _____

Exercise 4: THINK

A. Directions: Helen wrote this check to Ted's Gas Station. Look at it.

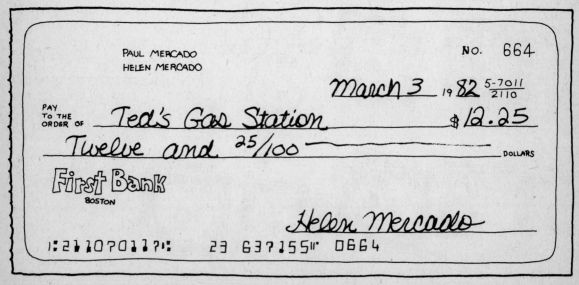

PAUL MERCADO
HELEN MERCADO

NO. 664

March 3 19 82 $\frac{5-7011}{2110}$

PAY TO THE ORDER OF   Ted's Gas Station $12.25

Twelve and 25/100 _____ DOLLARS

First Bank
BOSTON

Helen Mercado

⑆211070117⑈   23 637155⑈ 0664

B. Directions: Fill out these checks.

1. Write a check to Jim's Pharmacy for $9.32.

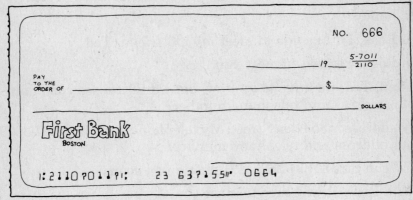

NO. 665

_____ 19___ $\frac{5\text{-}7011}{2110}$

PAY
TO THE
ORDER OF _____ $_____

_____ DOLLARS

First Bank
BOSTON

⑈2⑈⑈0⑈0⑈⑈⑈⑈⑈   23 6371551⑈ 0664

2. Write a check to the American Telephone Co. for $11.82.

NO. 666

_____ 19___ $\frac{5\text{-}7011}{2110}$

PAY
TO THE
ORDER OF _____ $_____

_____ DOLLARS

First Bank
BOSTON

⑈2⑈⑈0⑈0⑈⑈⑈⑈⑈   23 6371551⑈ 0664

3. Write a check to Sam's Clothing Store for $8.95.

NO. 667

_____ 19___ $\frac{5\text{-}7011}{2110}$

PAY
TO THE
ORDER OF _____ $_____

_____ DOLLARS

First Bank
BOSTON

⑈2⑈⑈0⑈0⑈⑈⑈⑈⑈   23 6371551⑈ 0664

LISTENING PRACTICE 1:

Ron: Hi, Ted. How are you?

Ted: I'm fine, Ron. How about you?

Ron: I'm fine, too. What are you doing these days?

Ted: I'm living in Cambridge now. And I'm working in a gas station. What about you?

Ron: I'm still living in Somerville, and I'm still working in the factory. My wife is working in the factory, too.

Ted: Your wife?

Ron: Yes, I'm married now. My wife is from Cuba. She's a Cuban. Her name is Rosa. I'm waiting for her. Here she comes now.

Rosa: Hi, honey.

Ron: Hi! Rosa, I'd like you to meet my old friend, Ted.

Ted: Hi, Rosa. Pleased to meet you.

Ron: Listen, Ted, we have to go now, but I'd like to see you again. What is your address and telephone number?

Ted: My address is 85 Glen Street. My telephone number is 447-3829. What's your address and telephone number?

Ron: 21 Webb Street. 391-2626. I'll phone you soon.

Ted: Good. Rosa, it was nice to meet you.

Rosa: It was nice to meet you, too. See you soon.

Ted: Bye, Ron.

Ron: Bye, Ted.

LISTENING PRACTICE 2:

Linda: Hi, Meg.

Meg: Hi, Linda. What's new?

Linda: My sister just got married.

Meg: Wow! That's great.

Linda: I'm looking at some pictures of the wedding now.

Meg: Can I look, too?

Linda: Sure. Here's my sister and my new brother-in-law.

Meg: She's pretty! And he's handsome!

Linda: Thanks. His family is big. There are his parents, four brothers, three sisters, and two grandmothers.

Meg: How old is he?

Linda: He's 27.

Meg: How old is your sister?

Linda: She's 24.

Meg: Are his brothers married or single?

Linda: Two are married, two are single.

Meg: They're all handsome!

Linda: Yes, they are.

Meg: Wow, I'd like to meet them. Can I?

Linda: Who? The single brothers or the married brothers?

Meg: The single ones, of course!

LISTENING PRACTICE 3:

A Telephone Call

Lois:	Hello, my name is Lois Gomez. I'm renting Apartment 10.
Landlord:	Yes, I know. What do you want?
Lois:	There are two problems in my apartment. I want your help.
Landlord:	What are the problems?
Lois:	First, the apartment is very cold. There is no heat. Right now I'm wearing three sweaters.
Landlord:	Okay, I'm listening. What's the other problem?
Lois:	This apartment is a two-bedroom apartment. I'm living here with my husband, two young sons, and two cats. And now my sister-in-law and mother-in-law are living here. So, there are six people and two pets now. We need a three-bedroom apartment.
Landlord:	There are no three-bedroom apartments in this building.
Lois:	Oh, dear. What can I do?
Landlord:	Read the ads for apartments in the newspaper. And ask your friends for help.
Lois:	Okay, but what about the heat?
Landlord:	What's the temperature in your apartment now?
Lois:	It's 68.
Landlord:	Sorry. The law says 68 is the right temperature.

LISTENING PRACTICE 4:

Marty: Hi, Doris. How are you?

Doris: I'm fine, Marty. How about you?

Marty: I'm okay. How are your children?

Doris: They're fine. They're in college now.

Marty: Oh, what college?

Doris: Nan is at Sawyer Business School. She's living at home. My son, Russ, is at Stanford University in California. He's living in a dorm at the college.

Marty: What are they studying?

Doris: Nan is studying secretarial science. She's going to be a secretary. At night she's working in a restaurant. She's a waitress.

Marty: What about Russ?

Doris: He's studying medicine. He's going to be a doctor. At night he's working in an office building. He's a janitor.

Marty: That's great. My daughter, Norma, is studying, too.

Doris: Oh, where is she studying?

Marty: She's at Boston College, here in Boston. She's studying nursing. She's going to be a nurse. At night she's a waitress, too — at McDonald's.

Doris: Is she living at home?

Marty: No. She's living in an apartment with two girl friends.

Alex: I'm going to rent an apartment. I'm going to look for it today.

Mike: You're living at your parents' house now. Aren't you happy there?

Alex: No, I'm not. there are too many people living in that house.

Mike: How many people are there?

Alex: Ten.

Mike: So are you looking for one or two bedrooms?

Alex: One. I'm looking for a one-bedroom apartment.

Mike: Where are you going to look?

Alex: There are several vacant apartments on Elm Street. There's one apartment in the building next to the liquor store. It's on the third floor, and it's not expensive. And there's another apartment on the second floor above the liquor store.

Mike: But there are several NO PARKING signs on that street. Where are you going to park your car?

Alex: I'm not going to park it on the street. There's a parking lot behind the supermarket. I'm going to park there.

Mike: Oh, there's a VACANCY sign in the apartment above Brook's Restaurant. Are you going to look there, too?

Alex: Sure, why not? Let's get going.

Mike: Okay.

LISTENING PRACTICE 6:

Lily: Every week I have to spend more money for food. Food is very expensive now!

Dot: I know. My family is very big. I have five children and my mother-in-law is living with us. My food is $125 every week.

Lily: Oh, that's a lot of money.

Dot: Today I'm not buying meat. Meat is very expensive. I'm buying chicken and eggs for dinners this week.

Lily: That's a good idea. I'm buying a lot of soup today. We're going to eat soup and sandwiches for dinner this week.

Dot: My family isn't going to eat in restaurants a lot. Restaurants are expensive.

Lily: You're right. We have to eat at home, too. But on Saturdays we can go to a cheap restaurant for hamburgers and french fries.

Dot: Well, I have to go to the checkout counter now and pay for my food. See you later.

Lily: Yes, see you later.

Mother: What a nice restaurant! We're going to have a good dinner here.

Father: I hope so. Here are the menus. Read them and decide what you want.

Tim: I want a hamburger and french fries.

Father: Hamburgers aren't on the menu.

Sally: I want a chicken sandwich and french fries.

Father: This is a dinner menu. Sandwiches aren't on the menu, either.

Tim: I have to eat a hamburger. I'm very hungry for a hamburger. I don't want anything else.

Sally: I have to eat a **sandwich** . I don't want a big dinner. I'm not very hungry.

Mother: Honey, this restaurant is very expensive. The soup is $2.50! I don't want to spend a lot of money.

Father: Okay, okay. We'll go to a cheap restaurant. Tim can have a hamburger and french fries. Sally can have a chicken sandwich. And I'm not going to spend a lot of money. What a crazy family!

LISTENING PRACTICE 8:

Mrs. Brett:	There's a sale tomorrow at Sam's. We have to go. Everybody in the family has to have some new clothes.
Mr. Brett:	Why do we have to have new clothes?
Mrs. Brett:	Jason and Jenny are going to start school next week. They have to have new clothes for school.
Mr. Brett:	What about me?
Mrs. Brett:	You're going to California next week with your boss. You have to have new clothes for your trip to California.
Mr. Brett:	What about you?
Mrs. Brett:	I'm going to California with you.
Mr. Brett:	Are you?
Mrs. Brett:	Yes, I am.
Mr. Brett:	Well, how much are you going to spend at the sale?
Mrs. Brett:	I'm not sure. Probably about $250.
Mr. Brett:	I'm going to go with you.
Mrs. Brett:	Why?
Mr. Brett:	Well, I have to buy some new underwear. And I'm going to help spend the money!

Nurse: Hello, can I help you?

Ted: Yes, I feel very sick. My stomach hurts a lot and my head is very hot.

Nurse: What is your name, address, and telephone number?

Ted: My name is Ted Briggs, my address is 312 Elm Street, and my telephone number is 267-5126.

Nurse: What's your age and date of birth?

Ted: I'm 36 and my date of birth is July 24, 1946.

Nurse: What's your occupation? Where do you work?

Ted: I'm a waiter. I work in a restaurant.

Nurse: Do you have health insurance?

Ted: No, I don't.

Nurse: Are you going to give me the money now?

Ted: Yes, I am.

Nurse: You can sit there.

PAUSE

Doctor: Hello, I'm Doctor Bell and I work here at Cedars Hospital. What's your name?

Ted: My name is Ted Briggs.

Doctor: Your temperature is very high. It's 103 degrees. How are you feeling?

Ted: My stomach hurts a lot and I feel very hot.

Doctor: Does your head hurt?

Ted: No, it doesn't.

Doctor: Does your stomach hurt on the left side or the right side?

Ted: On the right side.

Doctor: You are very sick. You're going to take this medicine and sleep at the hospital.

Ted: OK. I have to call my wife.

Doctor: You can call on the nurse's telephone.

LISTENING PRACTICE 10:

Pat: I want to rent another apartment. My apartment is small. It has one bedroom and a small kitchen. I want an apartment with two bedrooms, a kitchen, and a large living room.

Carol: How much rent can you pay?

Pat: I can pay $300 a month.

Carol: There's an apartment for rent on this street.

Pat: There's a FOR RENT sign and a telephone number to call for more information.

Carol: That's a new building. Where can you park your car?

Pat: There is a parking lot behind the building.

Carol: There's a telephone. You can use it to make an appointment.

PAUSE

Pat: Hello, do you have an apartment for rent at 19 Elm Street?

Landlord: Yes, I do.

Pat: How many rooms does it have?

Landlord: It has two bedrooms, a living room, a kitchen, and a bathroom.

Pat: What's the rent?

Landlord: The rent is $275 a month.

Pat: Does the rent include heat and hot water?

Landlord: Yes, it does.

Pat: Oh, that's good. I want to make an appointment to see it.

Landlord: Can you meet me there tomorrow at one o'clock?

Pat: No, I work every day. But I can come at night.

Landlord: Can you come at eight o'clock?

Pat: Yes. I'll see you tomorrow night.

LISTENING PRACTICE 11:

Marco: Excuse me, Mr. Kelly, I have to go to Bristol College. Can you give me directions?

Mr. Kelly: Yes, I can. First you walk three blocks to the bus stop and then you take bus 93.

Marco: Can you give me directions to the bus stop?

Mr. Kelly: OK. Walk straight ahead one block on Second Street to Elm Street, take a left on Elm and walk one block. Take a right on Fourth Street and walk one block to the traffic light. That's Bond Street. The bus stop is on the corner of Bond Street and Fourth Street.

Marco: Thank you. How long is it going to take to walk to the bus stop?

Mr. Kelly: It's going to take ten minutes.

Marco: That's OK. Classes begin at seven o'clock every Tuesday.

PAUSE

Marco: Excuse me. I want to go to Bristol College on Main Street. Is this the right bus?

Bus Driver: Yes, this is bus 93.

Marco: What's the fare?

Bus Driver: Fifty cents.

Marco: Here's a dollar.

Bus Driver: No, you have to give me the exact fare.

Marco: Excuse me. I don't speak English very well. I don't understand Please speak slowly.

Bus Driver: Give me fifty cents. I can't give you change.

Marco: OK, here's fifty cents.

Bus Driver: Go ahead and sit there.

LISTENING PRACTICE 12:

At the Pharmacy

Pharmacist:	Can I help you?
Mr. Todd:	I have two prescriptions. Can you fill them?
Pharmacist:	Yes, but you have to wait a few minutes.
Mr. Todd:	OK.
Pharmacist:	Mr. Todd, here is your medicine. It's in two bottles.
Mr. Todd:	Two bottles?
Pharmacist:	Yes. This is your first prescription. It is in a big bottle. You have to take two tablets three times a day. Take two tablets in the morning, two in the afternoon, and two at bedtime.
Mr. Todd:	Can I drive after I take this medicine?
Pharmacist:	No, you can't.
Mr. Todd:	Why?
Pharmacist:	It's going to make you sleepy.
Mr. Todd:	Can you refill this prescription?
Pharmacist:	No, I can't. First you have to see your doctor.
Mr. Todd:	I understand.
Pharmacist:	Your second prescription is different. It's in a small bottle. Take one of these tablets every day. Take it two or three hours after lunch.
Mr. Todd:	Why?
Pharmacist:	You have to take this medicine when your stomach is empty.
Mr. Todd:	Thank you. How much are they?
Pharmacist:	$18.56. Thank you.

LISTENING PRACTICE 13:

Registering for a Class

Jan: We want to register for night classes. I want to take typing and my friend Elena wants to learn English. She lived in Puerto Rico for nineteen years. She came to America in October. She doesn't speak English.

Secretary: Our typing class starts next week on Monday, January 11, at 6:30 p.m. It's a two-hour class and costs $65.00. The class is eight weeks long. The semester ends on Monday, March 1. Is that OK?

Jan: Yes, that's good.

Secretary: I'm going to ask you questions and fill out the registration form. What are your first, middle, and last names?

Jan: My first name is Jan, my middle name is Anna, and my last name is Blair.

Secretary: What is your address, telephone number, and social security number?

Jan: My address is 26 Elm Street and my telephone number is 235-1872. My social security number is 142-90-6378.

Secretary: When were you born?

Jan: My birth date is June 15, 1948.

Secretary: OK. Now, your friend's English class started last week, on Tuesday, December 30.

Jan: When is the next class?

Secretary: It's tomorrow, Tuesday, January 5, at 6:15 p.m. The class is ten weeks long. The semester ends on Tuesday, March 2. It's a three-hour class and costs $75.00.

Jan: That's fine.

Secretary: Give me your friend's name, address, and telephone number.

Jan: Her first name is Elena, her middle name is Maria, and her last name is Mora. Her address is 24 Elm Street, and her telephone number is 235-1732.

Secretary: When was she born? Where was she born?

Jan: Her birth date is May 29, 1947. She was born in Puerto Rico.

Secretary: Did she attend school in Puerto Rico?

Jan: Yes, she attended school for ten years.

Secretary: Thank you. You can pay next week. Good luck in your classes.

LISTENING PRACTICE 14:

At the Unemployment Office

Mr. Stone:	Can I help you?
Lil Costa:	Yes. I lost my job. I want to apply for unemployment.
Mr. Stone:	When did you lose your job?
Lil Costa:	Last week.
Mr. Stone:	What is your name, address, and telephone number?
Lil Costa:	My name is Lil Costa, my address is 37 Second Street, and my telephone number is 253-3893.
Mr. Stone:	What is your social security number?
Lil Costa:	279-42-1922.
Mr. Stone:	Who were your former employers?
Lil Costa:	I worked at Brook's Restaurant from January to March. Then I worked at King's Restaurant from March to last week.
Mr. Stone:	What was your job?
Lil Costa:	I was a waitress.
Mr. Stone:	Now I have to fill out this form. There are five questions. I'm going to ask the questions. Please answer yes or no.
Lil Costa:	OK.
Mr. Stone:	Did you work last week?
Lil Costa:	No.
Mr. Stone:	Did you look for work last week?
Lil Costa:	Yes.
Mr. Stone:	Did you refuse work last week?
Lil Costa:	No.
Mr. Stone:	Were you able to accept full-time work last week?
Lil Costa:	Yes.
Mr. Stone:	Did you change your address?
Lil Costa:	No.
Mr. Stone:	Good. Come here in two weeks on Wednesday, May 24, at 9 a.m. Then you can get your first unemployment check.

Paying Bills

Helen: We have a lot of bills.

Paul: I know.

Helen: The telephone bill and the gas bill came in the mail today, too.

Paul: How much is the telephone bill?

Helen: $49.52.

Paul: Last month it was only $24.00. Why is it so expensive this month?

Helen: I called my sister in California and you talked to your parents in New York.

Paul: Everything is very expensive. We owe $150.00 for the rent, $23.52 for the gas bill, $49.52 for the telephone bill, $75.00 to Sam's Clothing Store, and $53.50 for the electric bill.

Helen: I paid the bill for Sam's.

Paul: I went shopping this morning at Sam's and I bought a new coat.

Helen: Oh no! There will be another bill from Sam's next month!

Paul: I know, but I needed the coat. It was cheap.

Helen: I wrote a check at the gas station this week. My car needed gas and I didn't have enough cash.

Paul: We don't have enough money to pay all of our bills. We will pay the electric bill next month.

Helen: Next month is April. We have to pay our taxes on April 15.

Paul: I think we have to take money out of our savings account. I'll go to the bank tomorrow.

Helen: Last year we saved $500.00. We're not going to save anything this year.